THE MAHARANI OF ARAKAN

THE MAHARANI OF ARAKAN

A Romantic Comedy in One Act

FOUNDED ON THE STORY OF

SIR RABINDRANATH TAGORE

GEORGE CALDERON

Illustrated by CLARISSA MILES

Photographs specially taken by WALTER BENINGTON

GYAN

Published by

Gyan Publishing House
5, Ansari Road
Daryaganj, New Delhi-110002
Phone: 011-47034999, 9811692060
E-mail: books@gyanbooks.com

Distribution Network
gyanbooks.com
India, USA, Canada, UK, Australia, France

ISBN: 978-81-212-9142-2 (PB)
First Published, 1915

2nd Impression 2023

Printed at: Gyan Press, Delhi.

THE MAHARANI OF ARAKAN
AUTHOR: GEORGE CALDERON

THE MAHARANI OF ARAKAN.

From a photograph by Arya K. Chandhuri

SIR RABINDRANATH TAGORE

THE MAHARANI OF ARAKAN

A Romantic Comedy in One Act

FOUNDED ON THE STORY OF
SIR RABINDRANATH TAGORE

BY GEORGE CALDERON

Illustrated by CLARISSA MILES
Photographs specially taken by WALTER BENINGTON

Together with
A CHARACTER SKETCH OF
SIR RABINDRANATH TAGORE
Compiled by K. N. DAS GUPTA

LONDON
FRANCIS GRIFFITHS
34 MAIDEN LANE, STRAND, W.C.
1915

Staged by

THE INDIAN ART AND DRAMATIC SOCIETY.

CONTENTS

LIST OF ILLUSTRATIONS

A Short Character Sketch of Rabindranath Tagore

Rabindranath is our greatest poet and prose-writer. Son of a Maharshi (a great seer), and himself a seer, he belongs to a family the most gifted in Bengal in the realms of religion, philosophy, literature, and art. There is no department of Bengali literature that he has touched which he has not adorned, elevated, filled with inspiration, or lighted up by the lustre of his genius. The music of his verse and prose that fills the outer ear is but an echo of the inner harmony of humanity and the uni-

* This short outline of Mr. Rabindranath Tagore's life was written by Mr. Ramananda Chatterjee, the learned Editor of the *Modern Review*, on an occasion when Bengal seized the opportunity to do honour to her greatest *litterateur* on the completion of the fiftieth year of his life.

verse which exists at the heart of things, and which he has caught and made manifest to us by his writings. How wonderfully full of real life and colour and motion and variety they are! He has had access to the court of the King of Kings, to His very presence, and has brought us the message from thence:—"Be one with humanity, be one with all things that live, be one with the universe, be one with Me." Insight is his magic wand, by the power of which he himself roams where he wishes and leads his readers thither too. In his works Bengali literature has outgrown its provincial character, and has become fit to fraternise with world-literature. World-currents of thought and spirituality have flowed into Bengal through his writings.

But he is not simply a literary man, though his eminence as a literatus is such that for a foreigner the Bengali language would be worth learning for his writings alone. True it is that he is not an expert musician, but his musical instinct and genius are such that his musical achievements have often extorted the admiration of experts. We say this not with reference to his sublime and beautiful hymns or to his sweet and soulful singing, but in connection with what he has done for absolute music. He generally reads his addresses, reads in a way which few in Bengal have approached and none surpassed; but whoever has heard his extempore sermons and addresses knows what an eloquent speaker he is, though his delivery is often so rapid and his sentences branch out in such bewildering luxuriance as to make him the despair of reporters.

Those who have seen him acting some part or other in his plays of "Raja" and "Sharadotsab," those who have been privileged to hear him read his latest dramatic compositions, "Achalayatan" and "Dak Ghar," have experienced how natural and elevating acting can be.

His patriotic songs are characteristic. Some of them twine themselves with their tendrils about the tenderest chords of our hearts, some enthrone the Motherland as the Adored in the shrines of our souls, some sound as a clarion call to our drooping spirits, filling us with hope and the will to do and dare and suffer, some call on us to have the lofty courage to be in the minority of one; but in none are the clashing of interests, the warring passions of races, or the echoes of old, unhappy, far-off historic discords heard. In many of those written during the stirring times of the Swadeshi agitation in its prime he speaks out with a directness which is missed in most of his writings, though not in the "Katha-o-Kahini," containing, as it does, poems which make the heart beat thick and fast and the blood tingle and leap and course in our veins.

In his patriotism there is no narrowness, no Chauvinism, no hatred or contempt for the foreigner. He believes that India has a message and a mission, a special work entrusted to her by the Supreme Spirit, a special destiny. But he has never said that other countries have not their own special messages and missions too. He does not dismiss the West with a supercilious sneer, but wishes the East to take what it can from the West, not like a beggar without patrimony or as an adopted child, but as a strong and healthy man takes food and assimilates it. This taking, too, is the reception of stimulus and impetus, more than learning, borrowing, or imitation. He tells us in his writings that the West can cease to dominate in the East only when the latter, fully awake, self-knowing, self-possessed, self-respecting, requires no longer any blister or whip and leaves no department of life and thought largely unoccupied by its own citizens.

His hands reach out to the West, to humanity, not as those of a suppliant, but for friendly grasp and embrace.

Many there be who grow conservative with age. But Rabindranath is progressive and a practical social reformer.

His politics are concerned more with

character-building than with the more vocal manifestations of that sphere of national activity. Freedom he prizes as highly and ardently as the most radical politician, but his conception of freedom is fundamental. To him the chains of inertness, cowardice, and ignorance, of selfishness and pleasure-seeking, of superstition, of custom, of authority, of priestcraft, and of the letter of shastras, constitute our real bondage: the yoke of the stranger is largely a consequence and a symptom. This point of view has largely moulded his conception of the Indian political problem and the best method of tackling it. He wishes to set the spirit free, to give it wings—a largeness of vision; he desires that fear should be cast out. Hence his politics and his spiritual ministrations merge in each other.

Without any academic distinction or university degree, he is a highly cultured and extensively read man, acquainted with many of the best literary products of all lands. And now in the fulness of his powers he is thinking of learning the richest, in knowledge, of foreign tongues, and of again travelling in the West, to let in fresh light and air that can stream into the soul only through windows hitherto but partially opened. By the reading of books and periodicals he has always tried to keep his knowledge of contemporary thought up-to-date, to keep pace with its advance, with the efforts of man to plant the flag of knowledge in the realms of the Unknown.

As an educationist, he has preserved the spirit of the ancient Indian ideal, its simplicity, its avoidance of softness and luxury, its insistence on purity and chastity, its spirituality, its practical touch with nature, and the free play that it gave to all normal activities of body and soul. But in his open air school at Bolpur there is no cringing to mere forms, however hoary with antiquity. His mental outlook is universal. He claims for his countrymen all knowledge, whatever its origin, as their province.

By Annanda K. Coomaraswamy.*

Man has no body distinct from his soul. It would be difficult to exaggerate the significance for the Indian nationalism, of such a heroic figure as that of Rabindranath Tagore, the Bengali poet, dramatist, and music composer; for nations are destroyed and flourish in proportion as their poetry, painting, and music are destroyed and flourish.

The work of Rabindranath is essentially Indian in sentiment and form. It is at the same time modern.

Through all Rabindranath's song there runs an undertone of sadness: this must always be so in the work of serious men. This sadness is not gloom, but rather a secret joy that perceives with unfaltering vision the splendid pageant of life, but looks upon death as an adventure awaiting no less glorious achievement. One of the sweetest of the small lyrics, a four-line song to Death, might be a gentle, more feminine echo of Whitman's magnificent "Joy, shipmate, joy," just as the metaphysics of a poet recalls his "Terrible Doubt of Appearances."

DEATH.

Oh, Death, had'st thou been but emptiness,
In a moment the world had faded away.
Thou art Beauty : the world, like a child,
Rests on thy bosom for ever and ever.

Rabindranath Tagore's father, Maharshi Devendranath Tagore, was a leader of the Brahmo Samaj movement in Calcutta, a man of great personal piety and deeply religious. He was the heir to great wealth, all of which he renounced to satisfy the claims of his father's creditors, though not legally bound to do so. Rabindranath inherited his father's enthusiastic nature. Of a very sensitive, æsthetic, and mystical temperament, his nature reached to a very fine emotion, whether in life or art or religion.

Out of the materials of these emotions he has, to use his own metaphor, woven for his country a web of golden imagery, glorifying and re-creating her loveliness. Mysticism, the sense of the unity of life, is for him inseparable from the delight in all sensuous beauty: he is Vaisnava and Vedantist in one, believing, like Blake, that man has no body distinct from his soul, and the five senses are the chief inlets of soul in this age.

Two main influences affected Rabindranath in boyhood, that of his father and that of Vaishnava poetry. His father he accompanied on his widely extended travels to the Himalayas, and in the plains and by the rivers of Bengal. At fourteen he produced a sort of musical opera, called "The Genius of Valmiki." At seventeen he was sent to England, and studied at the University College, London, for a year. He visited England a second time without any intention of studying; his relations by this time despaired of his worldly prospects.

Returning to India, Rabindranath became almost a recluse. He lived for long periods in a boat on the Padma, the main stream of Ganga, in the Nuddea District of Bengal.

The profound influence of this lovely river scenery, which was for so long familiar to him, is again and again reflected in his poems and prose stories.

It was not till Rabindranath reached middle age—about forty—that his long period of growth bore fruit. Since then he has poured forth a veritable stream of poems, stories, plays, and other works; the keynote of which is the sense of the manifestation of God in the daily and elemental realities of life. His work, however, is not merely literary: he founded at Bolpur, in the West of Bengal, a school over which he still presides. In this quiet Ashrama, where classes are held out of doors under the mango trees, Rabindranath brings to bear upon successive generations of adoring students, the influence of his great personality. He thus exercises both a direct and an indirect influence upon the development of modern Bengali life and art.

The translations convey only a shadow of the original poetry, they give only the meaning; that in the songs themselves is inseparable from their music.

Some of them may perhaps convey a hint of the delicate charm of the originals and the perfect unity of thought with emotion that is expressed in them; but those who would really know them must understand their language—best of all, if they hear the poet himself recite them.

By Rev. C. F. Andrews.

There is one name which stands out far above all others in the history of the present Indian Renaissance—Rabindranath Tagore. For many centuries no such poet and musician has appeared in India. His songs and tunes are sung in crowded towns and remote villages in Bengal; and far beyond the borders of his own country his name is held in reverence. Already his poems have been reproduced in other dialects of India.

A short story will partly illustrate my meaning. I was once in a village in the heart of the great Himalayan mountains, not far from the borders of Tibet. A Bengali lad, about ten years old, had wandered up there, impelled by that roving instinct which so many Indian boys possess. Late one evening we were sitting in company with the villagers, when suddenly the Bengali lad began to sing one of the songs of Rabindranath Tagore. The dialect was strange to the mountaineers, but they could catch the drift of the words, and could feel the heart of the young singer going out in his song. They swayed backwards and forwards, seated on the ground, moved by the power of the song and stirred by deep emotion. So wide is the influence of Rabindranath's poetry and music in India itself.

The most difficult of all tests is now being applied to these songs of the East—the test of translation, not in fragments, but in complete volumes, into a Western tongue. A small book, called Gitanjali, has been the the first to appear, and its appreciation by those who are best able to judge has been whole-hearted. The poems have in no way suffered eclipse in their strange and foreign environment. They seem rather to have gained a new and added dignity. Stopford A. Brooke writes of them:—"They make for peace—peace breathing from Love. And because they all spring from union with undying Love, they appear in beauty —in a thousand shapes of beauty."

It needs to be explained in a parenthesis that Rabindranath's lyrical songs, such as those contained in Gitanjali, are not merely recited and read from a book. They are actually sung to music, and pass from mouth to mouth. This music, which the poet himself has wedded to his own verse, is frequently taken from the tunes of the boatmen and villagers of Bengal.

A friend of mine has described to me the scene when the aged Bankim (the greatest Indian novelist) was being honoured and garlanded at a gathering of the Bengali people. The old man took the garland from off his own neck and placed it on that of a young writer who was seated at his feet—Rabindranath Tagore. This act of Bankim's has since been universally recognised as worthy and true. For Rabindranath, as I have said, stands out far above all other moderns as the master-poet. What previous writers were struggling to attain, amidst almost insuperable difficulties, he has attained. The ideals of art, which the age before him dimly described, he has seen with open vision. Furthermore, he has inherited the prophetic spirit of his father, Maharshi Debendranath Tagore. He has arrayed his profoundest thoughts in a vesture of amazing literary beauty. His fame has come to the full in recent years, but his powers have clearly not yet reached their limit. His poetry has continually taken a deeper and more universal tone. It is leaving the precincts of Bengal and faring forth into the wider world. What the future holds in store for such a writer no one can predict.

But while Rabindranath's influence has

spread far beyond his own country, Bengal is still and ever will be the object of his love, the inspirer of his songs. What Shakespeare did for England in the days of Elizabeth, Rabindranath has done for modern Bengal. He has given vital expression, at a supreme moment in history, to the rising hopes of his nation. He has made Bengal conscious of its own destiny. In that country of music and song,

> "The prophetic soul of the wide-world,
> Dreaming of Kings to come,"

has found at last its appointed end in and through his poems. The dreams which young Bengal is now dreaming may not all come true; the glamour will inevitably pass away when this great literary age is over. But song and music are mighty instruments when the spirit of a people is beating high with hope and a master-hand can use them; and to-day men, women, and even little children, are seeing through the eyes of Rabindranath the vision of "golden

Bengal." That vision is luminous and radiant—the vision of a united people raised from the dust to sit with kings and princes. There is something about it which inspires religious fervour, and there is not unmixed with it also a feeling of religious awe and wonder—a rejoicing in the good tidings that God has visited His people.

Rabindra, lord of a new world of song,
  Heir of the sacred rishis of old time,
  This homage comes from a far distant clime
To hail thee crowned amid the immortal throng.

Whose words have power to make man's spirit strong:
  For thou hast reared a citadel of rhyme
  Great and majestic, with its towers sublime
Above the lower mists, which to this world belong.

Heaven sends to every people one pure soul,
  Filled with the spirit of music, who can sway

The hearts of countless multitudes, till they
Move at his bidding. Age on Age may roll
Voiceless, but when the singer comes, the whole
People awake to greatness. Nought can stay
The might of song on that victorious day,
When nations find at length their own appointed goal.

So wast thou sent to give thy nation birth,
Such was the power that brought back life again
To thy dear country. Like a gracious rain
Thy songs poured forth upon the weary earth,
And thirsting souls parched dry with arid dearth
Revived. The magic of thy mighty strain
Echoed in all men's hearts and swept amain
Darkness and gloom way, and wakened joy and mirth.

I have carried the manuscript of these translations (Gitanjali)* about with me for days, reading it in railway trains, or on the top of omnibuses and in restaurants, and I have often had to close it lest some stranger would see how much it moved me. These lyrics—which are in the original, my Indians tell me, full of subtlety of rhythm, of untranslatable delicacies of colour, of metrical invention—display in their thought a world I have dreamed of all my life long. The work of a supreme culture, they yet appear as much the growth of the common soil as the grass and the rushes. A tradition, where poetry and religion are the same thing, has passed through the centuries, gathering from learned and unlearned metaphor and emotion, and carried back again to the multitude the thought of the scholar and of the

* Sir Rabindranath Tagore was awarded the Nobel prize for literature in 1913. He devoted the entire prize of £8000, together with his share of the profits of the book, to the Bolepore School.

noble. If the civilization of Bengal remains unbroken, if that common mind which—as one divines—runs through all, is not, as with us, broken into a dozen minds that know nothing of each other, something even of what is most subtle in these verses will have come, in a few generations, to the beggar on the roads. When there was but one mind in England Chaucer wrote his *Troilus and Cressida*, and though he had written to be read, or to be read out—for our time was coming on apace—he was sung by minstrels for a while. Rabindranath Tagore, like Chaucer's forerunners, writes music for his words, and one understands at every moment that he is so abundant, so spontaneous, so daring in his passion, so full of surprise, because he is doing something which has never seemed strange, unnatural, or in need of defence. These verses will not lie in little well-printed books upon ladies' tables, who turn the pages with indolent hands that they may sigh over a life without meaning, which is yet all they can know of life, or be carried about by students at the university to be laid aside when the work of life begins, but as the generations pass, travellers will hum them on the highway, and men rowing upon rivers. Lovers, while they await one another, shall find, in murmuring them, this love of God a magic gulf wherein their own more bitter passion may bathe and renew its youth. At every moment the heart of this poet flows outward to these without derogation or condescension, for it has known that they will understand; and it has filled itself with the circumstance of their lives. The traveller in the red-brown clothes that he wears that dust may not show upon him, the girl searching in her bed for the petals fallen from the wreath of her royal lover, the servant or the bride awaiting the master's home-coming in the empty house, are images of the heart turning to God. Flowers and rivers, the blowing of conch shells, the heavy rain of the Indian July, or the parching heat, are images of the moods of that heart in union or in separation; and a man sitting in a boat upon a river playing upon a lute, like one of those figures full of mysterious meaning in a Chinese picture, is God Himself. A whole people, a whole civilization, immeasurably strange to us, seems to have been taken up into this imagination; and yet we are not moved because of its strangeness, but because we have met our own image, as though we had walked in Rossetti's willow wood, or heard, perhaps for the first time in literature, our voice as in a dream.

AMINA, THE MAHARANI OF ARAKAN

(Margaret G. Mitchell)

The Maharani of Arakan

A ROMANTIC COMEDY IN ONE ACT

The Scene is laid in Arakan, in the West of Burmah.

CHARACTERS

AMINA—A Mogul Princess
ROSHENARA—Her Sister
DALIA—The King of Arakan
TUNG LOO—An Old Fisherman
RAHMAT SHEIKH—A Mogul Officer
COURTIERS AND ATTENDANTS.

NOTE

Communications with reference to the Performance of this Play should be addressed to Mr Francis Griffiths, 34 Maiden Lane, Strand, London, W.C. The Play may be performed by Amateurs on payment in advance of a fee of Two Guineas for each performance.

The Maharani of Arakan

Scene:

Outside a fisherman's hut. AMINA *sits with household things about her, playing on a lute and singing.*

AMINA. Far from her land in a distant
strand,
In the shade of the Koilu-tree,
A maiden thought of her father's court,
Where once she was happy and free;
Ah, Princess! ah, poor Princess!
In the shade of the Koilu-tree.

(*Enter* TUNG LOO.)

TUNG LOO. What, what, what? Do you sit? Do you sing?

AMINA. What else should I be doing, Tung Loo?

TUNG LOO. Is it all done then, our work? The sun is halfway to the top, and my nets, no one has mended them; and the pots, no one has washed them. And you sit and sing foolish songs about Princesses.

AMINA. But what if I am a Princess? Must I not tell the truth even in a song?

TUNG LOO. An old story that. A Princess? How do I know? Is it written on you anywhere?

AMINA (*smiling*). I have a Princess' nature; I love to be idle and to let others work for me.

TUNG LOO. Ah, perhaps then Tung Loo is also a prince, for I like also to be idle; I like also to see others work for me. But in a fisherman's hut there is no time to be Princes or Princesses.

AMINA. This is no day for scolding, Father; look at the Koilu-tree, like a god of Peace in his robe of scarlet flowers which he sheds, like blessings, on the earth. Watch the reeds swaying gently as the little breeze plays among them. All nature is kind and gentle. Only men sit in the midst —always scolding.

TUNG LOO. That is true. Men scold,

TUNG LOO AND AMINA

AMINA. This is no day for scolding, father, look at the Koilu-trees, like a god of Peace, in his robe of scarlet flowers, which he sheds, like blessings, on the earth.

the sky smiles. Ah! But this is nonsense too. You talk sugar-talk; the old man sits and grins. Go and do your work, little water-rat.

AMINA. But to-day is a holiday with me.

TUNG LOO. Nothing to eat and nothing to drink, is that what you call a holiday?

AMINA. Dalia will work for us.

TUNG LOO. Dalia? For three days we have not seen your lover.

AMINA (*rising*). Lover? For shame! Dalia is my friend—my comrade.

TUNG LOO. Same word in Arakanee. And why is to-day your holiday?

AMINA. A messenger came at sunrise, a poor woman. She told me that my sister will arrive to-day.

TUNG LOO. Your sister? One day I looked at the river; I saw a log; I saw you on the log. I saw no sister.

AMINA. I thought that she was dead, that she was drowned. But now I find that she is alive. For two years she has been seeking me. At last she has found me.

Soon she will be here. Ah, then you will believe at last that I am of royal blood, when you see my sister. For Roshenara is a true Princess. She is proud and haughty. She will not let you talk to her as you talk to me.

TUNG LOO. Come, come, if she is a Princess, will she live by swallowing the wind? We want only still more dinner.

AMINA. I see you don't believe me.

TUNG LOO. Tung Loo believes everybody. That is Arakana custom. Now I go to mend my broken nets; you go to boil the rice, boil fish, make pleasant smell at noon, Amina.

[*Exit* AMINA *to house.*

You be good; Tung Loo be good; everybody be good.

AMINA (*looking out again*). But, Tung Loo, if I were really a Princess.

TUNG LOO. No more time for talk. Little fishes waiting to be caught; must not disappoint them.

[*Exit* TUNG LOO *to one side.*

DALIA ARRIVES ON A HORSE WITH RAHMAT SHEIKH TO TUNG LOO'S COTTAGE

AMINA *sings within, same song.* DALIA *arrives on a horse, with* RAHMAT SHEIKH; *he wears a royal robe and turban.*

DALIA (*alighting*). She is in the house. She is singing. Do you hear? Her voice is like the sound of a bell in a boat.

RAHMAT SHEIKH. It is a beautiful voice, your Majesty. It is like her sister's voice.

DALIA. Nonsense! It is like no other person's voice. Since first I heard her voice and saw her face, that is two years ago. Since then other women seem to me like nothing, only old tree-stumps. She has come, then, running away from Hindustan, she with her father, Shah Suja, and one sister, to the court of my father. I was wandering that day, very lazy, among bamboos in the garden. She went by with her women; no one saw me. She walked, she laughed. I wanted to laugh too. I said to my father: "I must marry that girl." My father said to Shah Suja: "Give me that girl, or I shall take her by force." Shah Suja said: "No, not either way." My father frowned, very angry. He said to some men: "Take them in a little ship with flags and music; throw them into the river." But that is all past and gone. He is dead; my father is dead. I am alive; she is alive; her sister too.

RAHMAT SHEIKH. Allah be praised. The Princess Roshenara.

DALIA. Tell me, Rahmat Sheikh, my people will be glad when they see I lead so beautiful a queen into my palace?

RAHMAT SHEIKH. When they are assured that she has royal blood in her veins, then they will be glad, your Majesty.

DALIA. Stupid people! Her blood she keeps a secret. She does not know that I know that secret. My blood, too, is a secret. She says to herself: he is a common man; he is a peasant. Rahmat Sheikh, do I look like a peasant?

RAHMAT SHEIKH. A king cannot look like a peasant, your Majesty.

DALIA. Stupid talk, Rahmat Sheikh. A king or any other man, he is all the same in the water. When the king has soldiers and a gold cloak, only then he is a king. Take this cloak please, and this. Are all things ready?

RAHMAT SHEIKH. The horsemen and musicians are hidden in a wood two miles from here, with the royal palanquin.

DALIA. That is good. Go and bring them here.

RAHMAT SHEIKH (*going*). It shall be done, your Majesty. (*Returning*) The great King is all powerful. . . .

DALIA. You want some other thing?

RAHMAT SHEIKH. When your Majesty is married to Princess Amina will you persuade her sister, the Princess Roshenara, to deign to look favourably on an humble officer like myself?

DALIA. If these things go well, you shall not be an officer, but a minister, my chief minister. You like that? That is good. Now, again I will be a common peasant-man. I want Amina to love me without my soldiers and my gold cloak. So now go!

RAHMAT SHEIKH. May the nightingale sit on your tongue!

[*Exit* RAHMAT SHEIKH.

DALIA *sings a song, "In the Bower of my Youth," then knocks at the door.*

AMINA. Who is that?

DALIA. It is nobody; only Dalia.

AMINA. Dalia!

DALIA. And these flowers.

AMINA. How lovely. (*Taking flowers.*) But come, sir, what have you been doing these three days?

DALIA. Ah, you have missed Dalia.

AMINA. Not at all. But I want to know what you have been doing.

DALIA. I have done nothing, only my work.

AMINA. Work? What work?

DALIA. All sorts of work—on my farm.

AMINA (Margaret G. Mitchell). Dalia, we are about to be parted for ever.

DALIA (K. N. Das Gupta). For ever? Oh, what a long time!

I have to feed my cattle and pigs. (*He laughs.*) That is farmer's work.

AMINA. You have been idling in the shade of the mango-trees, casting your eyes on the barbarous women of Arakan.

DALIA. Oh yes, twelve at one time. Shall I show you how? I take their hand so, then I take their waist so.

AMINA. Leave me alone, barbarian. Mogul women are not used to such treatment.

DALIA. We are not Moguls here, we are nothing, only Arakanees. You, too, you become Arankanee. In Arakan when we have not seen a friend for three days, we kiss.

AMINA. How different from Delhi! There we boxed their ears (*pretending to box his ears*).

DALIA. Ah, that is good too. You give me smiles. You give me blows. I say, it is all Doda. One day I had my arrows in my hand shooting birds. A white pheasant flew away. I said to my men: "I want that bird." They said: "She is gone; plenty left." Never mind, I want that bird. I went to get it.

AMINA. Did you succeed?

DALIA. Never got it. I followed that bird many days. In the mango-marshes very wet, in the sun very dry; everywhere nothing to eat. But thinking all the time of that bird. It is the same with Doda.

AMINA. Is that why you stayed away three days?

DALIA. Very busy, making a cage for a white pheasant.

AMINA. What do you mean?

DALIA. Only a white pheasant.

AMINA. Well, I have no time for riddles. There is no water in the house, and I cannot boil fish without water.

DALIA. That is true.

AMINA. So take these two pitchers and fetch me water from the spring.

DALIA (*holding her hands and kissing them as he takes the pitchers*). This is work I like to do.

DALIA AND AMINA

AMINA. Is that why you stayed away three days?

DALIA. Very busy, making a cage for a white pheasant.

ROSHENARA (Maisie Edmonston). At last I have found you, little sister!

AMINA (Margaret G. Mitchell). United at last—how happy we can be!

AMINA *looks after him and smiles to herself.*

AMINA (*singing*).

The bee is come and the bee is to hum
Till the heart of the flower comes out.
The bud says "yea," and the bud says "nay,"
She sways with a fear and a doubt.
O errant of wayward wings,
O guest of the sumptuous summer,
Give up thy hope, yet keep up thy heart,
O sunny day's newcomer!
Whisper in tearful tunes untired
And wait with a faith devout.
For the bud says "yea," and the bud says "nay,"
She sways with a fear and a doubt.

(*Enter* ROSHENARA *with a female attendant, who goes into the house with a bundle.*)

AMINA. Roshenara!

ROSHENARA. At last I have found you, little sister! How changed! A woman instead of a girl! And dressed in these poor rags.

AMINA. And happy in my rags. But tell me, you that I thought dead, how did you escape?

ROSHENARA. When the sailors fell upon us to throw us into the river, Rahmat Sheikh, our father's officer, hid me in the hold of the ship, and we stole ashore at midnight.

AMINA. United at last—how happy we can be!

ROSHENARA. But we must not forget the great duty for which Allah has preserved our lives.

AMINA. Duty? What duty is that?

ROSHENARA. Revenge!

AMINA. Oh!

ROSHENARA. Revenge for the murder of our father.

AMINA. But the king who murdered him is dead.

ROSHENARA. His son reigns in his place.

AMINA. But his son is innocent.

ROSHENARA. He inherits his father's guilt.

AMINA. I am his subject. I have my revenge by serving him.

ROSHENARA. You talk like the Christian books.

AMINA. Does not the Koran also teach us to forgive?

ROSHENARA. Princes do not know the word "forgive."

AMINA. But, oh ! must I take any part in this?

ROSHENARA. You more than any other, since it was in saving you from dishonour that our father lost his life.

AMINA. But what are we to do?

ROSHENARA. We must kill the king.

AMINA. But then they would kill us.

ROSHENARA. Are you afraid?

AMINA. To kill and to be killed is men's work. For me, I want to live.

ROSHENARA. To live? In a fisherman's cottage? Poverty was not made for Princesses.

AMINA. My poverty has taught me to know myself.

ROSHENARA. Is the daughter of Tamburlaine content to step down from the ivory throne of Delhi to a wooden stool in a barbarian's hut?

AMINA. I am a daughter of the sky and the land before I am a daughter of Tamburlaine. I am a woman before I am a Princess. Our family pride is a story of dead people. And the throne of Delhi is only a senseless block of dead elephant's teeth. Allah did not send me here to die, but to live, to breathe—to love.

ROSHENARA. To love? You cannot love in a country of savages.

AMINA. Why not? No, no. But if some prince of our own people should seek my hand. . . .

ROSHENARA. We have other things to think of now. Rahmat Sheikh is at the court of Arakan, spying an opportunity for our revenge.

AMINA (*laughing*). Rahmat Sheikh? A

tiger ready to lap milk from every man's bowl! But I am forgetting the dinner. Stay here a moment while I light the fire. Watch the river for Tung Loo, or I shall get a scolding.

(*Exit to house. Enter* DALIA *with pitchers of water. He comes behind* ROSHENARA *and puts his hands over her eyes.*)

DALIA. Tell me who I am.

ROSHENARA. Unhand me! Who are you that you dare to treat me so?

DALIA. What? So it is not Doda. I thought to myself it would be Doda.

ROSHENARA. Who are you, insolent stranger?

DALIA. Doda knows. Do you not know Doda?

ROSHENARA. No, I do not know Doda.

DALIA. And yet you sit before her cottage. (*Calling*) Doda. Is not Doda in the house? (*Enter* AMINA.) Ah, there is Doda.

ROSHENARA. That is my sister Amina.

DALIA. Your sister? No, that is Doda. Please, Doda, explain to us all who we are; explain to me who I am, and to this lady who she is, whether you are Doda or Amina.

ROSHENARA. I have been insulted by this man.

DALIA. But first let us know clearly who we are.

AMINA (*laughing*). Forgive me, I cannot help laughing. You are both so funny. I am Amina, that is my right name. And this is my sister, the Princess Roshenara.

DALIA. Oh, so now you are both Princesses. Ha, ha, ha, ha!

ROSHENARA. Who is this man?

AMINA. This man? One can hardly call him a man. He is more like a wild thing.

DALIA. Yes, more like a wild thing.

AMINA. He has no more sense than a deer of the forest. (DALIA *laughs.*) You cannot be angry with him.

DALIA. Nobody is ever angry with Dalia.

ROSHENARA. I have good cause to be angry with him.

AMINA. What did you do, Dalia? If he has done wrong I shall know how to punish him. Come, tell me what you did.

DALIA. I did nothing, nothing at all. I came here, I found nobody, only this lady sitting. I just put my hands over her eyes like that. I said: "Tell me who I am." But she could not tell. It was not Doda. It was nobody, only a stranger.

AMINA. What, sir! Do you dare to stand there and say such things?

DALIA. To stand there? Yes.

AMINA. Do you mean that you would have had the boldness to do such a thing to me?

DALIA. The boldness? To put my hands over your eyes? Oh, yes. No need to be very bold for that. Often I have played that game with you before.

ROSHENARA. Is this true, Amina?

AMINA. Sh!

DALIA. But when this lady looked at me,

so! Oh then, I was not bold. Oh, not at all. I was terribly frightened. Ha, ha, ha, ha!

AMINA. Did I not tell you the fellow was a boor?

DALIA. Yes, yes! Not a Princess, only a boor.

AMINA. Do you not know how you ought to behave in the presence of an Emperor's daughter?

DALIA. Not in the presence of anyone. I am nothing, only an Arakanee.

AMINA. Then you must have a lesson in manners. When you approach a princess, this is the way in which you must salute her. (*She salutes gracefully.*) Now imitate me!

DALIA. Imitate you?

AMINA. Do the same as I do. Salute my sister.

DALIA. Ah, that is difficult. How do I begin? (AMINA *shows him; he imitates.*) Ah, that is very pretty. I will do that again.

AMINA. Now let us suppose we are indoors—in a house.

DALIA. Indoors, in a house?

AMINA. Yes, let us suppose that this is the house, and that the house is out of doors.

DALIA. That is very difficult. That the house is out of doors, and that the out of doors is that house.

AMINA. Yes, that's right. (ROSHENARA *laughs.*) Now you have to take your leave.

DALIA. To take my leave?

AMINA. Yes, to go away.

DALIA. You say that I must go away.

AMINA. I say, let us suppose that you are going away.

DALIA. Oh yes, not really to go away, but only to suppose. That is good.

AMINA. Having made your salaam once, like this, you draw back three steps and do it again.

DALIA. Like this? Yes.

AMINA. And so you go right back to the door.

DALIA. Right back to the door?

AMINA (*pushing him in*). And through it. (*Laughing, she locks the door.* DALIA *looks out of a little shuttered window beside it.*)

DALIA. And what do I do next?

AMINA. You blow up the fire and make the fish boil.

DALIA. Is that part of the ceremony?

AMINA. The most important part. That will teach you not be impertinent again. (*She shuts the window. The sisters laugh.*)

ROSHENARA. So these are the friends you make in Arakan?

AMINA. One cannot live absolutely alone.

ROSHENARA. But the man knows nothing of the rules of behaviour.

AMINA. Oh, nothing.

ROSHENARA. And is it true that he has even dared to touch you with his hands as he boasted?

AMINA. What can you expect of an Arakanee? If we had been in Delhi and he had been the son of a Badshah or Nawab, it would have been another matter. But this is Arakan.

ROSHENARA (*laughing*). Come now, Amina, is it not a little this clumsy youth who has made the quiet life of the riverside seem so desirable to you?

AMINA. Why, sister, the fellow is a great help to me and Tung Loo. He brings us venison and game from his hunting; and does work for me that I find too unpleasant to do myself. I have done my best to teach him manners. But what can one do with such a man? Do you think he is angry because I have shut him up in the house? Not at all. If you look in, I have no doubt you will find him, with his face all scorched, blowing at the fire to make it burn and smiling all the time. What can I do? I am tired of trying to improve him.

ROSHENARA. I must see what I can do.

AMINA. No, no, you could only frighten him!

ROSHENARA. Are you afraid that I shall hurt your wild deer of the forest? No, no, I will not hurt him, for to tell you the truth, there is something in him that pleases me. Self-possession and good humour are more the mark of noble breeding than the observance of conventional good manners.

AMINA. Ah, now I see that you, too, are being won over by the influence of this peaceful scene. Is it not truly more prince-like to be a free woman, surrounded by the tranquil majesty of Nature, than to live enslaved in the traditions of a noble family, nourishing proud and revengeful thoughts?

ROSHENARA. You are half an Arakanee already.

AMINA. And you, you are not quite so Mogul as before?

ROSHENARA. A little less, child, from the spectacle of your simplicity.

AMINA. That is good, very good! (*They kiss.*)

(*Enter* TUNG LOO *hastily.*)

TUNG LOO. The seven powers of the

milky way preserve us! The King is coming here! His horsemen are all over the road; his messenger is at our doors.

ROSHENARA. The King!

AMINA. Do you not see, Father, this is my sister Roshenara?

TUNG LOO. Sister or no sister, what do I care? The King is coming, I tell you. (*Exit.*)

ROSHENARA. Do you understand, Amina, that the King is coming here?

AMINA. What of it? . . Ah! No! No!

ROSHENARA. See here is Rahmat Sheikh.

(*Enter* RAHMAT SHEIKH.)

RAHMAT SHEIKH. Salaam, O great Princess! I am the bearer of news. The King——

(DALIA *opens window.*)

ROSHENARA. We know your news; for what reason does he come?

RAHMAT SHEIKH. Princess, I will tell all, concealing nothing.

ROSHENARA. Speak on!

RAHMAT SHEIKH. Not long since the King, passing this way, espied the lady Amina at work by the waterside, and, fettered in the bonds of irresistible love by the spectacle of so much beauty, has resolved, after many days spent in passionate languor and exhaustion, to make her his wife.

ROSHENARA. Enough, Rahmat! Go tell your King that we will prepare for him a fitting reception.

AMINA. Roshenara!

(DALIA, *who has been watching this scene from the window, quietly closes the shutters and withdraws.*)

ROSHENARA. Sister, it is the hand of Allah, who rules all, that has brought him here. Our father's death in which he had no hand might have been forgotten and forgiven, but this last outrage never!

AMINA. Outrage, Roshenara? Is it an outrage to love me and to wish to make me his wife?

ROSHENARA. What? Are you truly a sister of mine? Grand-daughter of the

ROSHENARA AND AMINA

ROSHENARA. See, Amina, here is our father's dagger. Two years, night and day, I have borne it with me for the hour of our vengeance.

proud Akbar? Is it not an outrage that the son of the man who murdered our father should come here with his horsemen to carry you off, for a whim, a caprice, as if you were some peasant's heifer or she-goat which he had seen and coveted?

AMINA. But still——

ROSHENARA. Asking no questions whether you may not love and be loved by someone else already?

AMINA. Ah, that is true! He would separate me from Dalia. King or no King, I will not be treated so.

ROSHENARA. Now I see the true Tamburlaine blood in you! Come into the house. Let us array ourselves as Princesses should be arrayed for such a deed. And see, Amina, here is our father's dagger. Two years, night and day, I have borne it with me for the hour of our vengeance. It is a fitting weapon with which to pierce the bosom of the man whose father slew ours.

AMINA (*taking the dagger*). Ah, my Father's dagger. (*She kisses it.*)

ROSHENARA. Draw it!

AMINA. Yes, yes, it is very stiff. (*Pulling it out with a jerk.*) Ah, I was frightened.

ROSHENARA. Be brave!

AMINA. Yes, I will be brave. But, oh, to think that I must leave this happy scene for ever! This dear house, this river, and the koilu-trees that have sheltered me from the sun. And Dalia? Where is Dalia? Ah, he shall give me courage; he is a man. (*Opening the door.*) Where are you, Dalia? Come here. I have something very serious to say to you.

(*Enter* DALIA *with two baskets.*)

DALIA. I was shelling peas.

AMINA. Put that away.

DALIA. I can hear you with it in my hand. (*He sits down and shells peas.*)

AMINA. Dalia, we are about to be parted for ever.

DALIA (K. N. Das Gupta). And these flowers.
AMINA (Margaret G. Mitchell). How lovely!

DALIA. For ever? Oh, what a long time!

AMINA. The King has sent for me. He is going to marry me. I am to be the Maharani of Arakan.

DALIA. The Maharani of Arakan? Oh, what a grand person!

ROSHENARA. Don't waste your time with him, Amina; he understands nothing.

DALIA. Oh, Dalia great brain; he understands everything.

AMINA. But that is not all, Dalia. It was the King's father who killed Shah Suja, our father.

DALIA. In Arakan we say: he is dead, that is forgotten.

AMINA. That is not the way with the Moguls. You see this dagger?

DALIA. Why not? Am I blind?

AMINA. When I see the King I shall plunge it into his bosom.

DALIA. Into his—— Ha, ha, ha, ha!

AMINA. Do not laugh at that?

DALIA. Yes, I laugh. It is very funny.

The King sits there quite alive, quite happy. Up comes a lady, so sweet. He says: "O, my lotus flower." She says nothing, only Bom! What a surprise! Ha, ha, ha, ha!

ROSHENARA. Come, Amina. If this man had the heart of a mouse he would have offered to help us.

DALIA. Me? To kill the King? Ha, ha, ha, ha! It is too much you ask!

ROSHENARA. Coward!

AMINA (*kneeling*). Do you not understand, Dalia, if I stab the King his soldiers will stab me?

DALIA. Boum! Oh no, his soldiers will not stab you. That is not Arakana custom. (*Nibbling rice grain.*) Too much blood.

AMINA. What will they do, then?

DALIA. They drown you in the river; all water, no blood.

ROSHENARA. Come!

AMINA. I am ready, sister.

(*They go into the house. He shells peas and sings to himself, smiling.*)

DALIA. In the bower of my youth a bird sings,

Wake, my love, awake!
Open thy love-languid eyes, my love and wake!
There is a tremor in the midnight darkness to-night,
And the air is tremulous with the praise-song of Spring.
O, timorous maiden, blushing with the mystery of first love,
Listen in my grove of Paradise a bird sings in a repeated rapture,
Wake, my love, awake!

(*Enter* TUNG LOO.)

TUNG LOO. What are you doing here?

DALIA. I am shelling peas.

TUNG LOO. Make haste, then. The King may want to eat.

DALIA. No hurry. The King is not very hungry yet.

TUNG LOO. They are coming! Where are those silly girls?

(*Exit* TUNG LOO *to house. Enter* RAHMAT SHEIKH, MUSICIANS, *and* RETINU.)

RAHMAT SHEIKH. Your Majesty, why do you so demean yourself before the Court?

DALIA. To shell peas? Do they not eat peas? Only I am sorry I have not finished. Give me my robe, my turban. Not so comfortable, but very handsome. Ah, you salaam? I will teach you better salaam another day. (*Entering a palanquin.*) Let down the curtain. Hide my ugly face. (*Looking out.*) Fetch the ladies.

RAHMAT SHEIKH (*knocking at the door*). Oh, great Princesses, His Majesty the King, Maharaja of Arakan and suzerain of all the habitable globes awaits your pleasure!

(*Enter the* PRINCESSES, *richly dressed.*)

AMINA. Roshenara, Roshenara, is there no other way?

ROSHENARA. It is the will of Allah. Take the dagger.

AMINA. I had forgotten it. Good-bye, Tung Loo. Who will look after the little

Photo by Scott's Studio Ltd.

DALIA (K. N. Das Gupta). My soldiers are very strong men, but not strong enough to make you love me.

house when I am gone? Take this ring. Give it to Dalia. Tell him I loved him.

ROSHENARA. Be strong, Amina.

AMINA. I am ready.

RAHMAT SHEIKH. Most dread Majesty, the Princess Amina, daughter of the Great Mogul, attends your pleasure.

DALIA (*opening the curtains, and looking out with a smile as* AMINA *advances towards him*). Ah, is it my Doda?

AMINA. Dalia!

DALIA. It is not Dalia; no, it is nobody, only the King. (AMINA *throws down the dagger, puts her face in her hands, and cries.*) Did you think I would come with my soldiers to carry you off by force? What good is that? My soldiers are very strong men; but not strong enough to make you love me. Do you love me, Doda? Will you be my wife, Doda?

AMINA (*falling before him*). I love you, Dalia.

DALIA. Why do you kneel, Doda? The white pheasant flies over the hunter's head.

Give me your hand, Roshenara. Come and be a grand lady at the Court; teach us all good manners. And you, Tung Loo, you bring me a nice fish every day. I give you a piece of gold. Is that good? Will you give me that dagger, Doda? A wedding present to hang on a hook. An old story to make us laugh. (*He unsheaths the dagger a little way.*) See, the little dagger laughs too.

Dalia (K. N. Das Gupta). A nice wedding present to hang on a hook.

DALIA, AMINA, AND ROSHENARA

DALIA. Look, the little dagger laughs too.

AMINA'S FIRST SONG

AMINA'S SECOND SONG.

Words by Rabindranath Tagore

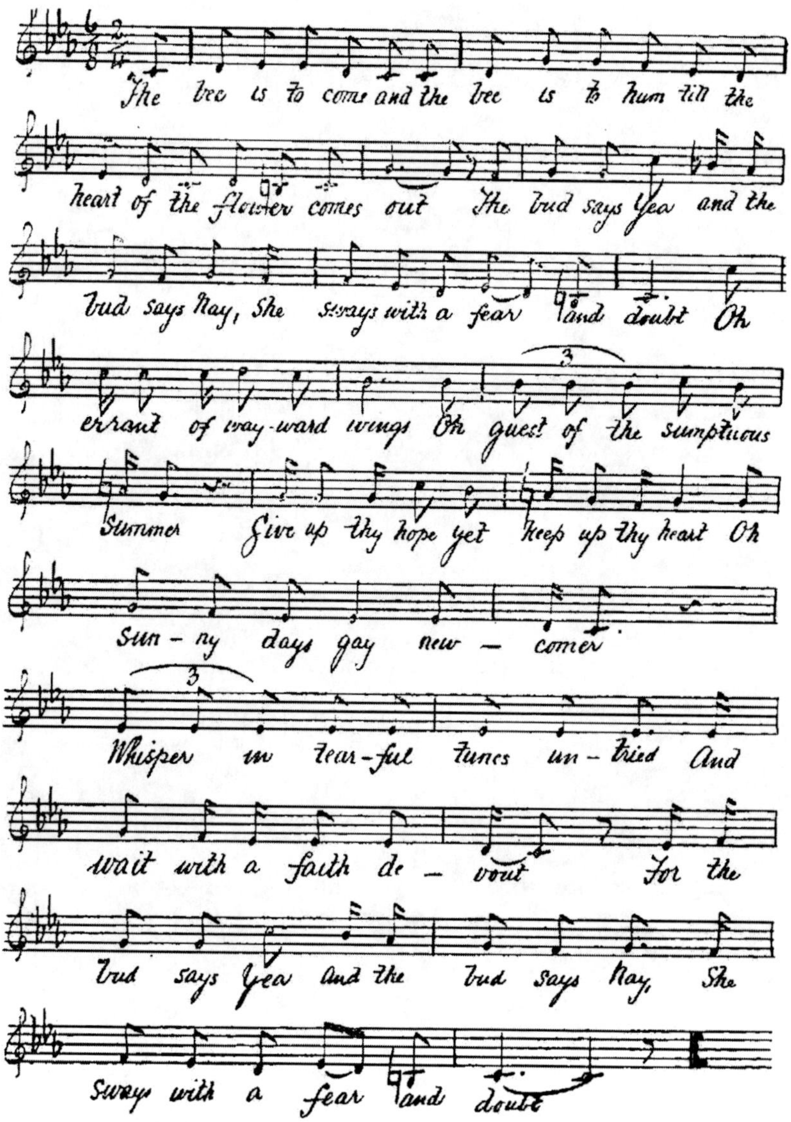

DALIA'S SONG

Words by Rabindranath Tagore

PRESS OPINIONS.

The Morning Post:—There can be nothing but praise for the romantic comedy in one act, "The Maharani of Arakan," Mr. George Calderon's adaptation of a story by the distinguished Indian poet, Rabindranath Tagore, presented at the Royal Albert Hall Theatre by The Indian Art and Dramatic Society, before a large audience, which found the piece entirely to its taste. The story, concisely, simply, and picturesquely set forth, deals with the love of Amina, a Mogul princess supposed to be a peasant girl. . . . . . The little piece, which is really well written, proved to be full of interest.

The Westminster Gazette:—The plot is very interesting, free from complications, and full of dramatic situations. The author's intention is to present an allegory upon the relations of Englishmen and Indians. India, like Shah Suja and his daughters, has fallen by fate into the hands of a foreign potentate; and just as the King of Arakan in the play foolishly endeavours to bring about unity by the exercise of despotic power, with the only result that it drives both the sisters away from his Court, and causes one of them, who has inherited only the pride of her race, to foster hatred and revenge; so, too, in India despotism on the part of England will never lead to good government and happiness. Moreover, in the play the evil is healed only when Dalia and Amina, casting aside the pomp of sovereignty and pride of race, meet in the common ground of simple humanity. So, too, England and India, by marching hand in hand towards common goal—the welfare of both races—will thereby bring about a final and permanent understanding and reconciliation.

The Times:— . . . . The little play gave an attractive picture of the fugitive Princess's life in the cottage of an old fisherman.

The Stage:—This excellent and daintily written little piece, although it deals with a rather trite subject, is full of interest and charm from start to finish, and certainly deserves more extended publicity than can be given it by isolated performances.